To Pete Still
with best wishes
J.W
Jan '86, Houston, Tx

NIGHTBLIND
Pamela Stewart

Raccoon Books, Inc.

Library of Congress Cataloging in Publication Data

Stewart, Pamela, 1946—
    Nightblind.
    I. Title.
PS3569.T4665N5   1985   811'.54   85-3555
ISBN 0-918518-47-4

Copyright ©1985 by Pamela Stewart

Raccoon Books, Inc.
Suite 401, Mid-Memphis Tower
1407 Union Avenue
Memphis, Tennessee 38104

Book and jacket design by David Spicer and Diana Taylor

ISBN 0-918518-47-4

ACKNOWLEDGEMENTS

Grateful acknowledgement is made to the following publications in which these poems, some in earlier versions or under different titles, have appeared:

The American Poetry Review: "Benediction," "Eurydice," "Gravity," "Insomnia," "Sea Longing," "Vespertine," and "Weather."
The Antioch Review: "Witnessing, the Pankot Hills, 1942"
Backwash: "Orpheus Transposed Among the Willows"
Crazyhorse: "I Was Watching and I Couldn't Stop"
Fiction International: "Local Color"
Harvard Magazine: "A Romance"
The Iowa Review (Extended Outlooks): "Postcard"
Ironwood: "The Sin Eater"
Painted Bride Quarterly: "A Formal Problem"
Planet: "The Twenty-Eighth Sailor"
Poetry Durham (England): "Cup & Saucer" and "H. D. At Karnak"
Poetry Miscellany: "Back Through Song" and "The Wind of Late Summer"
Porch: "Crime & Punishment"
Psychological Perspectives: "An Adagio for Hart Crane," "At Merlin's Grave," and "A Little Place"
raccoon: "The Eye of Heaven" and "Prothalamium"
The Seattle Review: "Spring"
Sonora Review: "The Estes' Backyard"
Telescope: "Nightblind"
Vegetable Box: "Staircase"

A number of these poems have also appeared in *Silentia Lunae*, Chowder Chapbooks, 1981 and *New American Poets of the 80's*, Wampeter Press, 1984.

I would like to thank the John Simon Guggenheim Memorial Foundation for their generous support which aided in the completion of this book. I would also like to thank John Barnie, Bob McNamara, Alane Rollings, David Spicer and David St. John for their critical attention and support.

For Katherine Hott, a way of meeting

"It is difficult not to be fictitious in so fair a place, but tests' severe repairs are permitted all."

—Emily Dickinson

CONTENTS

SPRING

The scent is back, a bridal weave
across the city. All night
the kiss won't leave our mouths
and memory steps, with dark measure,
between us and the flowers.

If we rise to this, the white
budded stars will shake,
the sky fall back to air.

I know what I've worn in my bones since birth,
hands at my throat, hands
at my knees, that swift red stain
between my teeth.

The future of memory flares.

We age, the flowers return. The trees I pass each day
fill up with birds. I pick
a single orange blossom which I crush to my wrist.

I could rub its skin to music, break
a man's bones to get to the heart.
I have only
one slow breath riveted to breath —

The stars stammer back their light
oil of flowers, bright enemy, heart.

TWELVE

The old black mine shaft had very clean
dark water. On a tufted
lichened ledge, above its endlessness,
a calf hung with one loose leg.
For a moment, the boy stared
into wider, more bewildered eyes
before he ran to tell his father.

All summer, the boy kept finding broken
useless things: a laced-up boot
in the hedge, a cracked pouffe
on 'Gwidden Beach, half
an open bottle of vodka
with three dead bees inside.
In August, a slack young gull
was liquid at both ends . . . .

These small unclaimed mysteries
began to pile like the half-read comics
tossed beneath his bed. Even that paper,
peeled from six jewel-skinned mackerel —
its terrible news of a boy just his age
found, body split and naked,
with flattened head — seemed part
of the holiday's insular progress.

His mother snatched and crumpled
the paper away as the fish softened
in vinegar's slow dissolving steam.

Today, he remembers that summer as a life between —
before he learned to desire the past
or yearn for a future. Those weeks
he kept stumbling on what he could do nothing about.
He's fifteen, and he's used to it now.

THE WIND OF LATE SUMMER

At first, what flew hard from my grandfather's mouth
into my mother's ribs was a feeling,
no more, no less.
Call it anger, call it love,
call it thunder cracking against the pines.

She never spoke of that moon looking up from the lake,
or the loons with their terrible noise.
The doorknob turned. His hands
became two red knots slipping at her breasts
while the wind rose on its hind legs.

Don't tell me I can't speak of this. My mother
hummed in her sleep as the mist off Sebago
sucked all light from the windows.
Grandfather stomped through the house
like it was still outdoors.

My mother wakes now over and over
to rattle about in the kitchen. She never thinks
of those sheets once pale beneath her storm-bound hair.
The house still stands in its timber.
It's August again, and wind brushes the pines

with the blurred sound of a girl's dress, torn
and falling. But Mother doesn't listen.

THE SIN EATER

Outside, the wind has not stopped. It tunnels
and the birds fall in.
The cabled shadow-and-sway makes a chill on my skin.

On the tables are trays, a chalice, and the long box
where he lies with his waxed, stitched-up mouth.
Small leaves are clicking at the window,
and tonight I am as far away from my name
as on the day it was given:

                          For it is not the cake,
not the pastries nor slabs of ham. It is not
that white fat rinsed in milk,
but how his lost breath pushes against me
a crumb of salt from love's encrusted feet.

The name of this man is hurting my mouth.
It's the name of my father,
a ladle of darkness between my ribs.
White stones flow from his eyes
and the wind
repeats his fingers tapping at the sill.

They have left me here, mortal and in love,
kneeling
to cradle the stones that must feed me.

HURT ISLAND

One house
is halfway up a hill.
A pocked August sun
superates
unkindly at the sill.

Beneath the stairs,
a child sways
humming, humming
while Father's face,
pummeled as damp new clay,

empties its blue
into an emptier day.
Whoever his wife is
leans at pots and pans.
She wears stained brown hands

difficult to kiss
and her knees scrape dry,
gristle to bone.
But tip to toe,
the specific child

goes twirling down the hall.
Against her chest,
a red rag doll.
She knows the world
is full of steam,

that it smells of chicken,
onions, greens,
that nothing shines

but the teething sea.
Above long tall dunes, clouds

extend their fish-spot hides.
This one day is always
a dank ancestral song:
Sunday's swollen liver
and all the house gone wrong.

A LITTLE PLACE

This world is a little place . . .
Hold hands, hold hands.

—*Charles Wright*

Mourning doves loosen the core of my throat.
Father, I am faithful
and never tell how birds can't even remember
flying violently up into leaves. Today
shadows shake the grit of their songs on the lawn.
But like you, such birds must forget
how they started everything over, and flew.

From the yellow eaves of this house
two pigeons shoot into the sun. What matters
is the way my eyes follow
and how desert sparrows stitch up the blankness
between grass and trees. I move closer
to touch that invisible seam
as your face pulls back into a little place.

Stupid, stupid ecstacy that tires my mouth,
I move closer without you.

A FORMAL PROBLEM

A wish makes up their dream
until the dream's long conversation
reshapes that wish. But this diversion
of husband and wife
is a mutual child pulling back the sheets,
until its parents say
"What have we made
from all this toss and fall —
is this really what, and where, we'll stay?"

Night to night, they sleep
kept from day's toughening light
until they separate in relief
and dreams walk back
into wishing's first need:
a man tending to his job, a woman
to her house, both to the small
gleaming hedges and walls
that daily bank their bodies in.

What is it, then, that begins to stir
as mortal dreaming comes apart?
In that white solid bed he touches
her slow thighs just to lose
her face and name, while she
lies in the crooked latch of his arms,
afraid her last wish — that he might die —
shines out, blank as prayer,
from her damp undreaming eyes.

INSOMNIA

Someone sleeps with his back to you,
or he doesn't. He sweats
as he dreams. On his lip
a small blue spot gathering clouds
beyond a mountain pass.

Miles from here, you see another man
staring into himself at the face of a woman.
She turns at the gate. He looks through her
right into the earth.

He wakes. You both wake. On the mountain
the deer stand betrayed.
One of them is you.
The sky loosens snow. A flash of hooves
circles your room, black spots
on the horizon.

In each hand you hold a story.
Between them,
your heart wedges into the earth.
Not flower, not mouth or star —
but an eye, half-shut, waiting.

GRAVITY

My mouth flicks into red points of air
as you hit me. A hand flies up
through mantles of space
I cannot fill or keep.

This is the bodiless night,
this is where innocence
frays along speckled air.

I touch one thread,
its pain
drifting from house to house.

    Ashes, ashes. Sleep while you can.

One of us falls. The children don't wake.
Their small arms and legs hold on.
I won't stay
though your heart, disembodied,
is sewn to my hair.

WEATHER

The room is torn
into a light you haven't dreamed of.
Clouds fall between two mountains
where blue deer graze.

You know this is true. You know
how his face has gone into rain.

The cat leaps to the sill
and curtains don't open.
Still, the light . . . .

The deer have slipped into a thicket.
He is miles from there.
How dark it's become.

The blue-nosed deer step near a pond
which fills with rain

and certain things are finally forbidden.
Low notes rooted in the corners, long
white hands folding paper.

The room is full of love
that may not remain.
The door is for these walls
that hold you. The door is for later.

I WAS WATCHING AND I COULDN'T STOP

I saw the door my friend walked through
beneath the chinaberry tree, and those windows

above bitten winter leaves
holding a perfect dusky hour. And this friend I love

kept walking in-and-out, and between
the voices of the women at the party. He kept

balancing particulars, his prophecies
and news. I had to smile.

His passion divided the world
for pure sense as he himself

became less pure. The sky darkened.
The voices, unloosed and pitching,

were too much for him. The windows,
starry and expressive, craved too much

as the moon's reductive chill
smoothed his face away. The door

thinned to nothing. So, as he wished,
no one could follow or love him enough.

BENEDICTION

for Sheila

In my dream, the man I am to marry
isn't the man I love in waking life.
It's the Colonel, your husband,
who years ago deftly murdered you.
I see you sit up, white-clad and dead,
to tell me how to care for him
while my horror-struck friends,
my mother and priest are screaming
How could you! Who would love such a man!
In the way of dreams, I've decided to.

I stand by the sea with his picture
in my hand. He is honey-hued
as the fogdog sun, with eyes
that blue-for-a-boy color.
It's dawn, the sea so flatly silver
I could be out in the middle of it.
I am separate
from the furious grief I've carried so long.
I don't care what this man is worth.
What calls from beneath my sleeping ribs
has me believe
I must take into my body and heart
that killer who took yours.

At the moment I wake, I know
I've moved closer to the man I love.
Though he's out trawling a real sea
we are not separate.
I dress, clear my head, brew coffee
while the Colonel hovers in the steam.
You, dead these four years, have finally risen.
We've forgiven your husband
and I don't mistake what I've taken in.
After all, what more can we do
before leaving this world, than choose
what to believe.

II

BACK THROUGH SONG

for Louise Bogan

All day, in the sound of soaking rain,
a woman leans against her desk
remembering
how the streets were once adrift
with wooden houses, how at dusk,
through open summer windows,
children would repeat their scales.
Long awkward songs plunged from the pianos.
Each day would hold unbearable promise,
and each night the secret reason for it.

In just hours, clouds break through
pink to grey. The pavement
holds that scent of freshly ironed cloth.
She locks her door and walks
across one street toward metal gates
that divide the world. There
children play inside the park.
They hoot and cry until a mother calls.
A ball thuds against a tree. Once, twice —
soft as fright.

WITNESSING, THE PANKOT HILLS, 1942

Rose-swell, before the monsoon, green
lost beyond green. The missionary teacher scrubs
white-washed walls, dress
lifted above her knees. Out of a London slum,
she has burned deliberate and true
waiting for these children.

One at a time, they enter the dim schoolroom,
open-eyed for the free chappatis. How simple
to show them England on the withered globe, to sing
"And did those feet in ancient times . . . ,"
making their eyes darken even more. Handing out
the color-your-own Bibles, she leans back
assumed such stories will ring true. Parvati,
the smallest girl who has never seen a crayon before,
reaches for the color blue.

"Suffer the little children" are words Parvati
cannot read, but beneath that fingering tree
she sees a man seated with open hands. She colors his face
cerulean with a bit of black. Christ's skin
turns blue. Parvati knows he's a god, that at home
on her wall Krishna's face takes the same hue.
Old Memsahib will be pleased.

All night a bell rings between the teacher's ears.
She cannot sleep. At dawn, she slips into the school
lifting, one by one, blue crayons from the shelves.
The year goes on. Rains arrive. Wordlessly
the children watch, having nothing
with which to paint any careless sky.

H.D. AT KARNAK

It's no longer the bright featuring
blood, no longer those brief

pure fires, nor your white skin.
It's no longer your burnished bones

and skull, but what's original:
not the visible body

at ease in this world
but that other which asks light

and song to rise. Tonight,
you stand in a doorway

watching the false gold recede.
Once it had stolen

your radiance but now is returned
to its first use and place.

A mystery makes known
no answer but itself.

There the light begins. Speech
begins. The mineral stars

bless and keep while birds
repair to your hands.

You have started such a long walk
to open this darkness.

Another love has touched you.
It holds an infinite steady shine

now that you are less
than perfectly beautiful.

AN ADAGIO FOR HART CRANE

Crossed as your gold-silted Florida Keys,
the world of the mind and the world of the heart
twine toward the pink childhood of conch.
Beyond this crumpled water, I imagine your dusky neck:
its half-blooded scent just a simple mist
to sleeve the arm or dampen hair. But closer now,
that blank dealt between love and more love
prowls the slope of years. For this

I linger and listen, hear the casting wind.
Is infinite meaning no meaning at all?
Beneath this lolling, smoke ridden fog,
I can't forget that there's another way
toward the uncertain wonder that quivers and chills.
It widens, cruel and melodic, both like
and unlike you splaying your innocent ten-fingered farewell
to signify what threads and weights, receives the eye.

HOUSEKEEPING

All a poet can do today is warn.

—*Wilfred Owen*

It's April in the air above my windowbox.
Hammers stun repairs into place
while women scrub their houses inside-out.
Washing my red winter sweater

in the bathroom sink, I see the water
filter pink then dusk to crimson
the way the blood from Jones' head
seeped across your mudslopped, khaki shoulder.

If you hadn't leaned at canal's edge
to help rebuild that bridge,
you might have lived to warn again,
to wash out your socks then later stroll

near a garden plot toward hyacinths,
or tulips, trembling in the twilit air.
Their gawky heads, still intact,
would dip and scan like that line of boys

stepping from a train in France.
But now I bend again, with elbows cocked,
to press the froth from sodden wool.
Knuckles and fingers repeat, repeat

how the truth that can't be kept from you
is in the steamy mirror
where someone familiar glances back
entrenched and useless, caught red-handed.

AT MERLIN'S GRAVE

I am thinnest where the pulling is.
Pressing my face against a tree,
I feel this charged ringing at my mouth:
web and water, web
of all the winds where edges meet.

The same thread
that spins raven to cloud
begins with grass, wind, rain
or the hour's desire. Listen —

bone, shell, no — skin of air
folds down toward wing
and in the charred ground, a seed.
How old this burning is
that makes me reach.

EURYDICE

I molt in the face.
The lake's skin
toughens this summer.

Yellow chintz hangs in the window,
water pulls along my eyes.
Yet you stand nearby
where I am not in love, and fire
fills the lake. Paper boats
sail off the island's lip.

I lived there once
as air above the flames.

There are times a man's torso
in the concave clench of love,
makes an animal-face.
At those moments, I must tell you

I am not air. I am just not.

But the boats have caught fire,
are dying in water. An edge
of yellow in my mouth, I bite down
hard. That face
surging in windowglass,
is it mine? Someone's opening the door —

I won't look.

ORPHEUS TRANSPOSED AMONG THE WILLOWS

Here now they walk together side by side,
sometimes he follows her as she proceeds,
sometimes he goes ahead and safely now
looks back at his Eurydice.

—*Ovid*

Orpheus dreams of willows draping the river
by that meadow where she died. How she gasped
with surprise, serpent teeth flashing
in the veins behind her knee.
Between worlds, she just looks at him. He wakes

as a severed thigh sings the blood-light
of an artery, its split
pomegranate of the many and one. Seeds
scrape his tongue. He hears her call him back,
for inbetween his world and hers,
she has no dominion. Rising once,
she opens wide her arms as the wind
throws itself from all directions

and she is driven down to that waiting room
where she sits
smoothing her skirt around two good legs.

*

Unlocking his throat, Orpheus stands
at his window and sees how the trees
beckon. Willow spikes are notation
against the sky. They teach him
all they know of exile: the speech
of animals and the one, many-sided song
no woman can resist. He knows
how she'll elude him if the words

go wrong, but trusts
the history of lyric far better
than her kiss. Even as she turns toward him
out of darkness, he cannot see
the soft trees falling through the mirror
of her weighted eyes.
The trees are full of love and from the deep
center of her reflection
she cannot believe his arms forget her,

cannot bear the dusky waiting much longer.

                    *

He washes his face in brackish water,
pulls tight his belt, rolls his sleeves
down against the chill. He whistles
and thinks how he will try for her
though he has no knife against the gods.
The throat of Orpheus is steep, walls
close in and what's lyric
has lost its melody of light. He can't
make out the gate until, suddenly,
like stars surging, he sees
her white knees shine. Those thighs
and two covered breasts he must not yet touch.
A shadow falls across his eyes
so he can't see her as she is, or imagine
what will be if they make it back alive.

                    *

He has found the word to keep a single
threaded note glowing in ascent. He thinks
again of willows, branch kissing slow
branch above restless water. But she's humming

beneath her breath. The air behind him
brushes up against his neck. *Would she dare
touch him just to die again?* He fears her,

for her, and who they are. They have sworn again
to release that death-star that's pulsed
for centuries inside their mouths.
Their last kiss forced it back
between her teeth and he must take it, now, away.

Fists deep in his pockets, Orpheus walks, singing,
so he cannot hear her, shrugs off
those long fingers at his nape, her gaze
burning between his shoulders. The song
pitches higher, weaves the world
inside-and-out to one note
that cannot tear. It seems *forever.*
His feet are stones, many and one, impossible
to lift until, stunned, a glimmer —
not moon, but a flaming cleft between boulders.
She claws his back, begs
that if he loves her now, to look! There

the river. Its signature catching sun!
Willows scrape the earth. He leans
across the bank that no longer
laments, sees above his watery face
her two eyes staring, silver, up at him.
Turning with a first awkward kiss, he takes
from between her lips that coin-cold star
and spits it into Lethe.
It flickers, sinks, and they walk home

together, safe beyond the shade of willows—
across the meadow
each deep in the shade of the other's world.

III

THE EYE OF HEAVEN

Brown sack hugged to my hip, I walk
home as wind lunges brightly around me.
Down the street, figs ripen
within the fingery green of their tree.
Suddenly, I hear the clacking arpeggio
of a fallen muffler. The car pulls up.

I turn as a Navajo boy jumps out, sees me
and grins. I grin back, eyes filling
with the shape of him: the spine's
knobs of light as he bends by the car,
his hair a black lowering globe of sun.
Just for a moment,
an impersonal lust raids the sky
and my eyes take all parts of him
until I wear

his brown, other skin as mine.

Back in the kitchen, no one is home
to talk to or touch. The sky
leaps against its light, then stills
with the weight of an incoming storm.
Birds stop
and low-bellied clouds fill with dust.

Rinsing lettuce and beans, I think
of how Dante said lust
is a lesser sin. How can I tell?
Those lovers, continually weeping, circle
a torn black sky. Mouth on mouth, they fell
into a war of winds

opening the eye of heaven.

But here you are with your hand on my hair.
The windows darken as across the street
figs swell and shine in the rain. We lie,
ankle to thigh. What limitless world admits us?
There are words not for my mouth. Caught
whirling in the eyelid of dusk, I cry

don't close, don't close until I must.

JACK YAZZIE'S GIRL

Dawn, with its scant plateful
of stars. From the west

brief flint-bright winds
whet their knives on stone.

Jack Yazzie pockets a handful of dry meal
and leaves his hogan. Small deer

might be waiting on the mountain.
But Annie won't wait.

She packs, and why not.
In the arroyo

old blackskirted women
claw flat water into pots.

They know how a day begins.
Thin-legged Annie shrugs past

the bird-pecked pools, the
clicking roadside lambs.

Thumb up, she strolls toward Gallup —
A trucker stops. Annie smiles.

His hand falls like dust
into her skirt. Deep

in the red-eyed barroom, Annie tilts
between tables that welcome any girl

who's left the flintblue air,
green corn, bony

ol' jackrabbit in the pot.
Outside, Orion buckles up his stars.

Annie shrugs, lifts
a glass of red water on fire.

LOCAL COLOR

A few hours, and already literature has tired my mouth
so I keep drinking in the loud-dim Lonestar Saloon
until Local Color moves in.
His stained boy's hand goes straight to my knee.
So drunk, I'd thought my knees had fallen off,
I'm startled as we leave.

Local Color's childhood still kicks at his ribs.
He drives a grey, beat-to-shit Plymouth
and I'm surprised that he has such long
white legs, like a pin-up. Local Color rolls his own.
He lives in a house beneath tall pines.

Like most men I've known, Local Color
was raised Catholic. With them
it's all or nothing, or just this side of maybe.
The one thing we have in common is *maybe* —
that space we press against with locked
faithless mouths while darkness spills away.

Local Color hasn't been to the dentist in years.
It shows. I've heard men of genius have bad teeth —
Rembrandt, Berryman, and young Stephen Crane —
all those torn hearts. But the local genius
of this boy's hands opens the window to stars,
opens me. Outside, the pines come green again.
The moon recedes.

       In this soft, local light
a blush rises from the sheets. Words
return to our awkward mouths. It's Sunday again.
And within that strict all or nothing,
is an elusive bright maybe

NIGHTBLIND

When that train's headlight veers
to kill my right eye, I panic
and the road goes black.
There are no white-line boundaries.
The radio croons "I can't
stop lovin' you," so I ask
each truck that passes to rescue me
back on course.

Aiming for their small red lights,
I name the drivers: Texas John
with a load of drills, Norman out of Tulsa
for Safeway again, and hailing
mud-splattered from Florida
is Skinny Bill "Truckin' for Jesus."

If I sit beside him high up in the cab,
he tells me he's moving pom-poms and batons,
and that it's God's will you're gone.
Then he lists the ways I should repent:
ashes, denial, prayer. Recalling
the brightness of your hand across my leg,
I can only say there's not one bit of evidence
I ever knew you. No bruises,
no address, no fallen threads of hair.

Steering by instinct, I get to that blank stretch
where mountains flatten
and stars pitch white along their edge.
I feel stupid with your name in my mouth,

or to claim that what is not seen
is even there. So stupid
that what I did see
was just loneliness crouched beneath your ribs
striking blindly out, within my arms.

VESPERTINE

Now light falls out of the garden
unchaining its trees
and blossoms still. A wedged sky
deepens purely.

I know that God moves in
to break our hearts
so we may choose reshaping them.

These are the words you told me,
the no-words
unfolding from the face of wall.
I touch my mouth, my tongue.
I touch the air a bird went through.

The dog, barking down the street,
is certain of his purpose.

There's a crack in the walk, a spider's husk

and far across the world, rooms
with iron bars
are calling down the night.

CRIME & PUNISHMENT

After all, it was bloodless until now.
The anarchist, with his loop
of piano wire running just one red seam
across the clouds, was hardly believable.
I will not go out again. Long
blue shadows cross the hillside, seeping
closer. They force a boundary
between the victim & his blood.
If he bleeds, we may never know it happened
until the shades evaporate along the hills
with a red metamorphic snow that will be final.
Last time, I put the corpse in a suitable garden.
Springtime flourished & I veiled myself
in lacy hysteria that tricked the flowers
into bloom. My great-grandmother's bequest?
A necklace of tiny jeweled skulls, for each
a jar of seawater buried in the yard.
The problem was with the original spells.
I should have laughed them off
but was enthralled instead:
cover this one with your breath & he
will find you. Paste this one to your inner thigh
to protect you from disease; the green-eyed one
for unlikely luck. And this? Keep against your throat
to stop the water rising. Beware
of others like ourselves
& always keep these hidden. But I am lying again.
I forged the chain myself from the gulley
of a dream. It was filling with water, & maybe
the chain of skulls pulled me in. I'm still paying
& think I must be stopped. I think
the jars must be broken, & then a ribbon
placed around my throat to hide that red
wire mark, emerging now from years ago.

A ROMANCE

Soft and thin, your eyebrows are the brushstrokes
of my loss in winter: characters of snow
opening this chapter against my legs
and up into the deep
tunnel behind my eyes that searches endlessly
for you. I talk further into the dark now,
sometimes flaring
above those sockets I've promised to kiss.
One day a cage went looking for its bird,
found you in flight. The effortless
green bars closed around you. Seed
spilled across the floor, pointillist
as the snow piling outside
my imaginary window. And with it now
its burden of inexpression
called *love.* You wipe your hand

across your cheek with the fever
of a boy who opens a door
onto a woman sleeping naked in summer.
It's that same breathless heat
a criminal feels before his first crime
as he plots his exit, the taxi stalled in snow.
A gate slammed shut. The woman turns
onto her side, hair damp at the neckline.
She, too, dreams of you, the doors, and snow
possible on your shoulders three years
from now. But inbetween, a continent
of bureaucrats disallow any
heartland weather. Each year they repaint
the cages stacked in a row, lean back
to admire their banded birds. They cannot see

your eyebrows, or your teeth gone angular
from grinding in the night. The enamel
punctuates your mouth like bits of ice
you swallow halfway through this story:
its long dream of snow falling
into the darkened slope of woman,
into her hair,
feverish as our love, helpless as its crimes.

PROTHALAMIUM

They've thrown us in jail:
me inside the walls,
you outside.

—*Nazim Hikmet*

I have opened the door; there's a wind outside
that changes everything. I might be home
by a pond at dusk, the sharp
rain-scented wind rising to stir the water
and my hair. This is the first breath
of autumn in the desert. My cat bathes
in the window-air as mulberry trees
toss into darkness. This wind holds
the wordlessness of beginning again. A gesture
that, after sleep, climbs the long days.
I am certain only that the cat stretches
feeling all of herself, and that my hand
is here, yours, somewhere else. All of this
because the wind reminds me of home
and of a pond I might show you where the same wind,
surprised, finds us walking uncovered by rain.

*

Didn't we once ride horses together?
There was a hayloft's secrecy, the vacant
air we swam through. The uncut field
trampled to mazes. We shared those rooms,
the knife and the contraband Luckies in childhood's
alliance. Here, in the Visiting Room, our eyes
meet, slide, meet again. And they foolishly
call us lovers . . .

*

The pond has opened its eye to summer. Weeds
at the edge darken their green. They stir.
The tree frogs are blending their songs
for tonight, just tonight, and there
are the fireflies I always promised you.
The field, rimmed with birches, goes dark as the pond:
an eye widened to take both our bodies in.
How pale we are at dusk, your leg stretched
all the way along mine
under this spring-fed northern water.

*

I used to sleep in a house guarded
by a wall of pines. They loosened snow
from their dark centers. It piled
onto the steps and sills. On a mountain
I own in my mind, snow blurs everything now.
Your face flickers through the dense
white. Breaking through that opaque cold,
I see iron bars close hard
behind you. Your shoulders gone in a blizzard
beyond my reach. I dress for winter,
a vigil under guntowers that will seem
forever, but really is not. See, there I am
in a red cap and jacket. Like that hunter
who's left his gun at home, I wait
to see just how thick the snow falls
and what stranger
will walk vividly back out of it.

*

Remember, you dreamt of the room? Its
table and chairs, two windows? Here's
something that resembles it. Behind my eyes

are yours: pine boards, resin-dark, the white
quilt bunched in a corner. Like flying,
our arms rise and fall
to spread out the bedding. Shoes
abandoned, your hands press
at the window as a thrush brings round
our first evening home. The purple lid
of sunset dimming behind the ridge.
I told you it would be like this, once
at least. And now you look hard into my face
for the mirror I carry — its infinite
silver passage that we carefully tend

despite the fat,
brown-shirted man who taps your shoulder again . . .

STAIRCASE

in memory of Richard H. Rovere

The day you died I was visiting a prison, kissed
someone not unlike your son, felt home
in the cruelest place. My hand,
still with bitten nails, draped shyly
across the chipped blue divider. All around me
paint was peeling, families leaned into each other
locked hard in the cliché
that life is precious. When the gate slammed
behind me, I was seventeen and homeless again.

At seventeen, I'd wanted your house
and leafy sunlight, the magical curve
of that bannister where my ragged adolescent hand
felt so elegant I became an important lady.
I'd been welcomed, and ever since
have desired those yellow summer roses,
the guestroom's marble sink, and that staircase!
I was in love with your family. I read

your books, kissed your son, knew nothing.
From my desk I now see the grey book
you gave me, in German, about that con-man
Joe McCarthy. You smiled at me. I guess you thought
I'd learn the language, grow up, return.

In Arizona, mulberry trees occasionally shake
a few yellow leaves, and the low built houses
have no staircases. The prisons
have tiers and metal steps that shudder
when someone is carried to an unmarked grave.
I think how even momentary families are precious
and how much we forget
until a slap of sunlight or a black-bordered page
brings us home again. In that hollow behind my eyes,
the staircase slopes toward and away from you.
I reach for it and what it meant, thinking
I'm sorry. I still want it all.

THE ESTES' BACKYARD

I never saw such a place as this
for always being there. Even the weeds
have gilded pink and yellow heads
glamorous as promises, and the citrus trees,
Chaplinesque in their white-washed trunks,
lean as though to dance away.
I used to think of settlement as death,
but here the orange blossoms sink their weight
like lovers close to a tense blue sky.

My cat, in her first springtime chase,
attacks a white ceramic duck. Its beak,
lifted and always dripping,
is frozen by the genius of this place.
Beneath one grapefruit tree, a painted
Mexican pot fills with twisted leaves, and caught
on an abandoned web, a single
white blossom splays like a woman's tibia
shelved in some canyon dwelling's loss.

Because of luck I may touch this world,
be touched. My skin opens to a drench of light
where something has taken me in
while those I love, living and dead,
pull closer to the surface of this earth.
I call, one by one, the ghosts

of chance affection up while blocks away
a man returns from work
to sudden, empty rooms and a siren
makes tremulous the heavy bridal scent
enclosing the city. Yet nothing
hurts the moment of this place.

Neck stretched back, I see the garden
with its chaste, roseate wall slip
behind my eyes. The ghosts
fall into shadow, hushed by leaves.
And, like air, my spirit clears
in this given careless green: original
as that which promised me the world —
heartlessly perfect.

IV

POSTCARD

Dusk, the sea is between colors
and our medallion star is ready to leave for China.
This is the brushstroke hour
you have already befriended.

I am here for the first time
taking a rush of water into my mouth.
My ribs fold with a white salt weight.

Centuries ago, Mu Ch'i slipped his eye
from fog to indigo. A grain of sand
dislodged from a monastery wall.

His six bitter orbs of fruit
are still blindingly pure.
And everyday
his seventh, unpainted persimmon
ripens across the sky.

The bell-blossom moon follows behind.

Here, in California, the day shakes once
and falls. The ocean pulls closer.
With luck, you say,
a sudden streak will flash toward the stars

as the flaming persimmon dips into salt.

In this way the eye will complete the day.
It will root in the heart.
My hands return from water, the water
returns from China.

I would unstain my heart to carry it with me.

THE OLD COUNTRY

Light rains into the body of the sea.
There's an east wind, and that wide song
the water makes. I'm amazed
at how long the sky has been this perfect a blue,
at how the sun clamps onto everything:
cobbles, granite steps, the brown
oiled bodies of women and children. Even the boats
relume their reds, blues, unlucky greens — briefly
romantic until, moon-driven like us,
they too shall be dispossessed.

I'd thought my first summer here
would be wet and grey, an indoors-solitude.
I can hardly stand this white
indecipherable burn at the edge of the sea.
Over and over, something breaks
against me, over and over
the distances take me in. For you never know
how it comes on you — love —
why, injured but persistent, it stays to sing.

AT ZENNOR POINT

I wanted, walking, to be not
myself but part
of slope and sea: bracken, thorn,
the gorse-starred cliffs —
salt-smitten air
above that scatheless green.

But they and the wild white sky
resisted, the shape of wind
and wave resisted —
so my only self was otherness
that wished aloud
and cared, or directed any word.

SEA LONGING

St. Ives. The streets are sighing
in their salt-damp, vertical stone.
I can hear the tide's
incessant thunder as our sky twists
with such a wind it blisters the stars.
When you were five and first went to sea,
I was spending absent, air-borne eyes
on books and imaginary friends
until all my world filled in.

But your white-shouldered world
has mutable edges, the sea
her own desires. Once, nets shot over,
a rope coiled around your leg
and you went too, down
with just a caught breath
between your ribs. Knife quickly drawn,
you managed to cut through
until you soared violently upward
into the borderless air.

Now wind is pulling along our cliffs
as the salt-and-holy water of St. Eia's font
rides out to where fish are waiting
for the silvery reach of your nets.
It's a daily business, like love
and questions of faith. You and I
touch and separate at the will of the wind.
Knowing this
love keeps returning to itself, like the sea.

for E.

AGAIN

Within the gloved dusk of a hill high
above the Pacific, a man steps out
onto his porch and hugs himself
against the wind. Mourning doves
whirr in the pepper trees and the sea
is very wide, falling green to black.
This man is remembering how, at times like this,
he dislikes the sea and so returns his heart
to that slow river unspooling his childhood
from its silt-brown cradle. How often
he'd float there beneath bunched watery stars
and reach for the blue
tribal dead swiveling in their wind-cloud
chairs. Far away,
at the lip of another sea, a woman
leans above a sink, its basin filled
with cabbages and beans. Again,
she imagines the small motion
between that man's ribs, the pulled
drape of his jacket bathed
in the peach and tin of California twilight.
Once she's loved him with the honed
distant passion of a girl, a clear
foolishness that delivered her to other men.
Sometimes, he'd say how the wind held voices,
one meant just for him. He'd listen hard all night,
at dawn, or in the brawl of winter rains.
But whatever tale the wind began for him

in riverbank sleep refused to finish
by the open sea. Last night the woman dreamed
of the one time he'd touched her
in a yellow room at dusk. But now
she lives on a shoreline loosed far
from rivers where a rough wind
is always speaking. She knows
the end of its story, of the strict
resemblance of dream to sorrow.
On this side of her solitude, she means
to tell herself how glad she is
that a certain man never loved her back. Not once.

CUP & SAUCER

for Becky Roach

Little flat water, little
water that pretends it isn't the sea.
Clear, just dusted water
in its tea-set sibling shapes.
The trackless sand settles.
This is where children find private season
between fallen primrose
& the blackberries' white
cut-out stars. This is where
limpet shells hold fast
& the water is warm. Basket & towel
are tossed away while, naked,
a girl stretches her first body out
& grins to be the Saucer's spoon.
In the Cup, a boy jumps up & down
shouting all of himself for her.
Sometimes they splash each other
to salted bloom, or chase
a lucky stone toward ferns. Here,
at low tide, these pools keep house
for children, but
in harder weather repair to sea.
As the children grow, their arms & legs
must buckle to fit
so they move to other summer things.
The girl, fiery & dark, now

fashions tarts and cakes. The boy
works hard his boat, makes man-wet noise.
The water waits all of its seasons.
Tourists swarm the cliff path, dogs
clatter about to piss
& there are fewer water-skinned children
for this place. Genderless as memory,
the worn shapes remain
half-used, the way a man & woman late for work
leave dishes on the table. What spills
is a little water, twin
to little flat water waiting for the sea.

PSYCHE

As a child, she used to ride apple boughs
like horses, or power. She'd kiss
the shiny pitted leaves, the skin-pink blooms
that were the meaning of summer
as they hardened, then swelled to fruit.
Each year, as the trees toughened and grew,
she'd rock-an'-roll her way through love:
books, boys, radio tunes. Today,

in a church where strict and beautiful wooden saints
stare down from a ceiling that's arched
as a woman ready to conceive or bear,
there is a pure stasis in the way she looks back
up into their forbidding painted eyes. They ask
how much more of herself can she take, how much
of last night's whiskey-light and smoke, that man's
long thighs pressing against her?

Again, she's lurched into a season
where the far off sin of longing has started
to flower. Its dark whisper nuzzles her ear,
its mouth falls along her as all
the small town talk and dirt sting her eyes.
Those trees that once possessed her have been cut
to logs and burned. Some of those saints, who had
real bodies, have also burned. So many hard bones

of lovers have turned into something else she cannot
name except to say she's still falling, still
soft and falling for no reason but the want
of that man who held open her coat, then kissed
her eyes and throat. They didn't speak as they walked
through dark prying streets, past the church, out
to the new and laden streets where no children sing
or weep, and only stars stare blankly down — burning.

THE TWENTY-EIGHTH SAILOR

Tonight the wind keens high, like a widow
bereft of name. As I stagger against this black
Biblical air, the sea roils and sucks.
Flung churned foam makes hill and trench
along the drabbled beachside homes.
This storm, so clearly Cornish, invokes
the Reverand Hawker in his claret-
colored coat and tatty jersey
with the Cross sewn in above his heart.

How he'd brace himself for that grim
succession of drowned sailors
littering his coast. Even shapeless
dismembered limbs were hauled up the cliffs
to his lych-gate house. All that, and
the muttering cluck of women dying cloth
for shrouds, drove the Vicar to his hut. There
he still kept watch for corpse, or poem,
armed with just paper, quills, drops and spoon.

His twenty-eighth sailor — lean, handsome,
face unlined — wore thin elastic boots
and never was identified. Poor
irascible Hawker never could refuse
any broken body that was his charge. He never
hardened his heart despite the demon weather,
the countless desecrated bones
and scraps of skin in earth and water.

The wind batters and screams. The sky
tightens while stars unloose

from their hopeful moorings as though the galaxy
still contracted in pursuit of Hawker
who buried that sailor in the afternoon
then turned, stricken,
to learn that a woman digging for bait
found a severed right foot
on the beach at Coombe.

THE DAMAGED ARIA

You stand at cliff's edge thinking
Look at all that sea! (That's nothing, that's
just the top of it.) The sea finds, takes
then forms herself again. At dawn, she'll be
as glassy and silver as a lover's thumbprint
dragged along sex-moist skin. The skipper's eyes
clench with such deep white fires
from having looked straight into the wind,
into that solid spray and light. Then
the weariness of too much wanting
lessens in a deceptive chant of waves.
How often, in our hearts, we fare
just that shoreless, indefinite as God . . .
And when, with precision and fury, the sea
claims cargo, iron, wood and men to seed
their ornament and bone across her hidden floors,
we may know nothing of it. We simply say
they've disappeared as, sky-sheeted
and at peace again, the sea lies back down.

———————

We're catching up. Our inventions
are closer now to God's. You know how rooms,
streets, cities wear their damage — not just
as accessory, but as style — how levees,
a bloodied shirt, or broken books remind us
of the body wrenched from its ideal?

Today, the hummingbird bruise below a cashier's eye
is all too familiar.

When the original song gets away from us
it hurtles, singlemindedly, forward —
or clear back to Merlin crouched beneath Peredur's tree:
There, still rising, is half a spray of moist

green leaves, the other side on fire.
From the hidden clefts of seeds, our first
passion splits to embers and early snow. Look —
beyond the ancient hills, now breaking,
just infinite oceans of steam.

———————

What the world says is a birdnote,
what it throws across two lovers
is a long quill of original light.
Hope has no house but this woven air.
It calls the walking fires
from the swamps, lifts wind-bitten thorns
to shelter lambs from cold. Up
through the beaded center of lakes, cities,
hearths or the sea's own bed, it links
root-laced ancestral faces back to us.
No more than a reed can help the wind

from blowing through it, this world
is a world of facts. The day,
grey or blue, is yet itself
and the damaged aria with its firm white tongue
still yearns to sing clear through,
and from within, the only selves we have to use.

for Dana Weimer

NOTES:

The Estes' Backyard was inspired by Donald Hall's essay "The Continental Drift."

The Twenty-Eighth Sailor: Robert Stephen Hawker, 1803—1875 — poet and Vicar at Morwenstowe on the north Cornish coast. I should like to thank Robert Peters for introducing me to Hawker, and for urging me to visit Cornwall.

Witnessing, the Pankot Hills, 1942: After an incident in Paul Scott's *The Raj Quartet.* (Not the film version.)